FAITH IN A BARREN LAND

TRISH M

© 2013, Trish M Enterprises

ALL RIGHTS RESERVED.

This book contains material protected under International and Federal Copyright Laws and Treaties. Any unauthorized reprint or use of this material is prohibited. No part of this book may be reproduced or transmitted in any form or by any means, electronic or mechanical, including photocopying, recording, or by any information storage and retrieval system without express written permission from the author / publisher.

Cover Design: Design Studio

Interior Design: Trish M Enterprises

Cover Photo Composite: Damion Dunlap Photography

Editor: Carol Thompson

ISBN: 978-0-9897064-0-7

DEDICATION

This book is dedicated to the man that I have spent more than half of my life with…my high school sweetheart, my rock, the one who helps me to be a better me each and every day of my life. I wouldn't want to go through any barren land with any other person but you by my side. You are my strength. Thank you for being a wonderful husband, father, and friend. The love that I have for you is indescribable. May God bless us with our forever. I love you so much!

ACKNOWLEDGMENTS

First and foremost I must give honor and glory to God. Without Him, I wouldn't even be here to share the joy of the Lord which gave me the strength to overcome and live long enough to tell somebody else how they can do it as well.

Again, to the love of my life…my always and forever…my rock, my husband… Mr. Derrick Morrissette, whom I have spent more than half of my life with. I love you so much.

My two beautiful children, DaeShaun and Daesha….after reading this book, I hope you have a better understanding of what it took for you all to manifest in our lives. You two were definitely worth waiting for. I can't begin to tell you how much of a miracle you are to us. We love you so much.

Mommy (Jeraldine Dickinson), daddy (Danny Dickinson Sr.), and my five brothers (Myreon, Eric, Danny Jr., Greg, and Damien respectively), thank you for the love and support, and for helping me to be the woman that I am today. I love you so much.

And last, but certainly not least, to all my family and friends who have been there by my side…I love and appreciate you so much.

CONTENTS

Introduction: Life's Lessons	11
Chapter 1: Faith	15
Chapter 2: A Barren Land	23
Chapter 3: Barren Land #1- Finances	27
Chapter 4: Barren Land #2- Infertility	37
~ The Journey Continues	51
~ Third Time's The Charm???	53
~ Fourth Try…Grace Us Lord!	59
~ Can We Do It Again?	67
Chapter 5: Barren Land #3- Spiritual	71
~ Overcoming Spiritual Barrenness	77
Chapter 6: New Level of Faith	81
~Scriptures To Strengthen Your Faith	89
Chapter 7: Overcoming It All	99
~ Inspirational Quotes For Being An Overcomer	107

Pray Often
WORK HARD
TRUST GOD

INTRODUCTION

LIFE'S LESSONS

I have learned over the years to simply trust God. Having faith when times are hard seems like one of the absolute hardest things to do…but yet will I trust Him!!! When things start going downhill, I trust Him. When blessings and prophetic words aren't manifesting, I trust Him. When times are hard, guess what? I trust Him!

As I look back over the years, I think about all the things that I have gone through. I think about all of life's situations. I think about being in that land of barrenness, where it seems like everybody is getting blessed but me, and I had to ask God, "Why me Lord? Why am I going through all of this? Why won't you bless me like you blessed such and such person? What do I have to do to get a breakthrough?" I must admit, I had to learn how to walk in the fruit of the spirit. Not just part of the fruit, but the entire fruit. That fruit consists of love, joy, peace, patience, kindness, goodness, gentleness, faithfulness, and self control. I didn't know how to love myself the way that I should have been loved because I was always comparing myself to others who were getting blessed. I always looked at myself as maybe not being good enough. Or perhaps, maybe

God doesn't love me as much as the next person; therefore, loving myself didn't go very well during this time and season of my life. And, what about joy? How can you be joyful when it seems like you're not being blessed? Yes, I put on the mask, but the reality was that I wasn't. I didn't have peace. I was disturbed in my spirit as to why I couldn't get to that land of milk of honey…my very own Canaan….my very own promise land. I knew that God had blessings waiting on me, but I became very impatient in that process of waiting. What must I do Lord? What must I do? I remember nights of weeping; nights where I began to lose faith as to whether my dreams would ever come true. I couldn't control the tears. I just knew that my life was incomplete. I knew that God could turn my whole situation around, but why hadn't He?

I knew that I had to write this book so that I can share my testimony. I went through many seasons of barrenness, but the Lord brought me through it all. I know that there are so many women out there who have gone through something similar, but I came to give them hope. I came to shed some light on this process that they have or may have to endure.

Being faithful in the middle of the storm can be hard, but yet doable. My prayer is that after reading this book, you will be empowered to embrace the process that God has you in. Don't quit. Don't give up because it will take faith in a barren land to get you to your promise.

CHAPTER 1

FAITH

We hear so often… "have faith, be faithful, God is faithful, trust God…" It's easier to say, but so much harder to do when you are going through the trials and tribulations of life. What exactly does it mean to have faith? What is faith? Well, if we look at Webster's Dictionary, it will tell us in one definition that faith is "The belief in the facts and truth of the Scriptures, with a practical love of them; especially, that confiding and affectionate belief in the person and work of Christ, which affects the character and life, and makes a man a true Christian, – called a practical, evangelical, or saving faith." Dictionary.com describes it as "the trust in God and in His promises as made through Christ and the scriptures by which humans are justified or saved." If we go to the word of God in Hebrews 11:1-3 KJV, there we find that faith is "the substance of things hoped for, the evidence of things that are not seen." So, in a nutshell, having faith is believing that something will happen even though it doesn't seem like it will, or at that moment, hasn't happened.

If we believe in those things that aren't current at the moment, then we exhibit hope for the unknown. We continue to pursue our ideal happiness without giving up on it. Though we can't see it, we dream it, we visualize it, and we imagine what our lives would be like with it in our existence. Having faith gives us a reason to pursue our dreams, our happiness, our quality of life. Image if there was no faith. What would this world be like? Imagine if there were no hope for tomorrow… no hope for change… no hope for prosperity… no hope for increase… no hope for a better life. I can only imagine the unfruitfulness of the land. To have faith means that you live with the expectancy that things will be different, that a change is going to come. Faith is so vital to those of us who are called Christians because the word of God tells us that without faith, it is impossible to please God (Hebrews 11:6). Faith is such a powerful gift of God that he said in his word in Matthew 17:20 "So Jesus said to them, 'because of your unbelief; for assuredly I say to you that if you have faith as a mustard seed, you will say to this mountain move from here to there, and it will be moved. Nothing will be impossible for you.'" We know and understand that this is not a literal statement. Christ is not talking about you literally going up to a mountain and picking it up and throwing it somewhere else. No!!! No matter how large your faith is, this is not the point that he was trying to make. What he was saying is that the power of faith reflects the omnipotent nature of God who bestows faith on his own. The mustard seed is one of the smallest seeds, so the amount of faith needed to do great and mighty things is actually pretty small. Jesus clearly makes the point that little is much when it comes from God.

Some believe that by saying they have faith, it is an automatic thing. However, having faith is far more than just a belief. It is an action and a choice. Much like love, we are given a choice whether to put it to work or leave it sitting on our Christian shelf. Christianity has no room for shelves. It is not about trophies to put on display. Faith is believing, but it is believing and then putting that belief into action. The Bible tells us that "faith without works is dead" (James 2:20). For example, suppose you believe in your heart of hearts that God promised you that you would have your own business and that it would be prosperous. Well, step one has been accomplished. You start your own business, but you fail to follow up. You fail to strategize. You fail to execute properly. Then, you no longer believe that God wanted you to start the business so you decide to close shop. You fail to realize, that yes, God promised it to you, but there are certain things that you need to do to position yourself for the prosperity that was included in the promise. Again, as just stated, faith without works is D E A D. So take the time to put in the work to get to the abundance that God has proclaimed to you. Let's look at Abraham for example. Abraham was one who embraced the promise of God. God told Abraham at an old age that his wife would conceive and bring forth a child in his old age. Abraham believed God, and it was credited to him as righteousness (Galatians 3:6). Abraham heard what God had spoken to him. He understood that his wife would conceive even in their old age. Abraham also understood that to get what God had for him, he had to go home and put in some work… meaning he had to go home and make love to his wife. He didn't let his current situation dictate whether or not he would receive the blessings of God. Abraham could have easily made an excuse for why he couldn't go home and have sex with Sarah. Let's be real. It's not that easy for a man that's about one hundred years old to say, "Well, I think I'll have sex with my wife today." Abraham chose to put in the work to achieve the blessing that God had promised him. So how does this apply to your life? If God made you a promise, figure out what you need to do to see it made manifest. Don't sleep and slumber claiming that you were waiting on God. God is saying that he's waiting on you! You're not waiting on God. To receive all that God has for you, go ahead and clock in your faith AND your works…. pull a double! Show the enemy that you will do whatever you have to do to get ALL that God has for you.

    I know without a shadow of doubt that faith is about believing, but it is also following through in action. Believe that God will meet you there and provide for you in your faith. You might not know exactly what to do, but you go by faith, and believe that God will give you direction and guide your every step. You see, much like when Jesus called Peter out of the boat, He had faith that it was Jesus calling Him. But it was not true faith until He got out of the boat and walked toward Jesus. It took him not only believing, but also acting on that belief. Even when He failed, Jesus was there to catch him.

So what exactly can your faith do? If you truly believe without a shadow of doubt and you activate that belief by putting in the work, then your faith will allow you to do what many in the Bible did and even more. Your faith can manifest God's healing power in your life. If you are believing God to be completely healed from any form of sickness or disease, then look at the story of the paralytic in Mark 2:2-5, 10-12. The paralytic and his friends knew that if they could get to Jesus, then he would be made whole. The crowd was so thick that they couldn't get past them. They knew that if they put in the work by climbing to the roof top, tearing it off, and lowering the paralytic down in front of Jesus, then he would be made whole. When Jesus saw this, He told him that his faith is what made him whole. They were willing to tear the roof off of a building to get to their blessing, and their faith is what caused the paralytic to receive the wholeness in his body.

When the storms of life are raging, did you know that your faith can calm the storm and bring peace in the middle of the chaos? In Mark 4:35-39, we see the calming of the storm by Jesus Christ himself. When the winds were raging, all Jesus did was speak the words, "Peace be still." Just imagine what would happen if we chose to do what Jesus did. The word of God tells us that we will do even greater things than He did! We have to use the authority that was given to us and speak to those situations, those trials, those tribulations… we have the authority to also say "Peace be still" and see our whole situations change just like that! It's called a faith walk. You have to believe that when you speak into the atmosphere and demand for things to line up according to the word of God, then a shifting has to take place. You have to believe that you can do all things like calm storms through Christ who gives you the strength to do so.

One thing is for certain. According to the word of God, we will be able to do even greater works than Jesus did (John 14:12). But it is going to take faith, whether the size of a mustard seed or not, to achieve this. This means that whenever we or a loved one has issues, our faith is what's going to cause the situations to change. Whenever there is sickness, we should believe by faith that a simple laying on the hands will make one well. When there are financial problems, we speak the word of God that the enemy is rebuked for our sake, especially when we know that we are tithers.

Bottom line, no matter what season you're in, you have to operate in faith. You have to put in the work to receive all that God has for you. You have to understand that even though you don't see it, it's on the way. You have to speak into the atmosphere. You have to believe by faith that it is so and it is done in Jesus name. You have to walk it out completely and fully knowing God will bless you and make your way prosperous. Challenge yourself to go to a new level in your faith walk. You'll see the difference that it shall make in your life.

CHAPTER 2

A BARREN LAND

Covering faith is one thing, but talking about a barren land is something else. What exactly is meant when we say "barren land?" Well, if we look at Dictionary.com's definition of "barren," it will tell you that it's, 1) "not producing or incapable of producing offspring; sterile: *a barren woman*, 2) unproductive; unfruitful: *barren land*. 3) Mentally unproductive; dull; stupid, 4) not producing results; fruitless: *a barren effort*, and 5) destitute; bereft; lacking."

If you are going thru a season where you feel that your land is barren, then you may be one who is trying to have a child, but you are finding that you are having fertility issues which cause a barrenness of the womb. Or, you may find that you're in season where you're not very productive. You may feel like you're not accomplishing your hopes, dreams, or your desires. You may feel as though you're mentally drained, mentally unprepared to do what you know you need to do in your heart. You may find that your efforts are barren because you're not getting the results that you want. To say that you are destitute is saying that you are lacking what you need to go forward in the things of life. So, what can you do to deal with all of this barrenness?

If you want to overcome your barrenness, you have to gain authority and power over not being fruitful no matter what area of your life it is. You have to make up in your mind once and for all that you will be productive, you will be fruitful, and you will overcome at whatever you set your mind to do. God tells us in His word that we are more than conquers (Romans 8:37), that we overcome by the blood of the lamb and the word of our testimony (Revelation 12:11), that we can do all things through Christ who strengthens us (Phillipians 4:13). So, why is it not happening when we want it to happen?

We have to realize that God allows us to go through seasons of barrenness for a reason. It's not because He wants to see us hurting or suffering; however, it is ALL for His glory. Just imagine if we never had to go through anything! Then, we wouldn't have a testimony to help someone else. Then, we wouldn't be able to tell somebody of the "goodness of Jesus and all that He's done for me." If we didn't go through the test, then we wouldn't have the testimony; no mess, no message; no trial, no triumph. In these next few chapters, you'll get a chance to see how both you and I, can and will, have triumph as we go through seasons of barrenness.

CHAPTER 3

BARREN LAND #1- FINANCES

I remember the day so clearly. I was excited about finishing my studies at Troy State University in Troy, Alabama (now called Troy University). I had gotten a double major in Spanish and English. I purposed in my heart to double major to make myself more versatile in the business world so that perhaps I could receive multiple job offers in different areas. Mission accomplished! I was so excited about the job fair that was being held on campus for that year's graduates. I had my resume and portfolio all ready. I knew that I would find the perfect position somewhere.

During that time, my husband and I had just gotten married. He finished the semester before I did and was already working at an auto parts company. We had already agreed that we would be open to moving to whatever place gave us the best offer. He would simply transfer his job or get a new job. Ok, agreed.

That day, I met with several recruiters who gave different proposals for me to come and work with them. There was one gentleman in particular whose offer stood out just a little more than the others. This man had made me an offer to come to Panama City, Fl to teach Spanish at one of their local high schools. The salary wasn't as high as the other offers that I had gotten, but I entertained it because he added an addition to my salary. He told me that if I would come, they would even have a position in the school system for my husband (who, by the way, had gotten his degree in Psychology). So, my husband and I had the opportunity to go to Panama City, Florida, and we would both work in the school system making decent salaries; or so we thought.

I was extremely excited about the offers that were made to me on that day. I went home that afternoon anxious to tell my husband about everything. We narrowed our decision down to two locations- Panama City, Florida and Dallas, Texas. Dallas made a pretty nice offer. The salary was a LOT more than Panama City; however, the only downside—they didn't offer a position for my husband. So, we eventually decided not to go to Dallas. Panama City would soon be our home!

Upon arriving to Panama City, Fl, we soon realized that the cost of living was extremely expensive in comparison to Troy, Alabama. The rental fee for an apartment was five times higher in Panama City! You would think that the salaries would be a lot higher because of this.

Once we got to Panama City, we soon realized that we were manipulated and deceived. There was no position for my husband; only me. We were promised a moving stipend and sign on bonus. We never saw the moving stipend, and we had to continuously remind them of the promise for the signing bonus!

Mind you, we were a couple of young adults just starting out in life. We didn't think about putting ALL these promises in writing because we were too excited that they were even made to us in the first place!

We constantly reminded them of our bonus, of our moving stipend, of the promise to hire my husband. As time went on with no job for my husband, bills continued to pile up. They wouldn't stop coming. Bill collectors calling… one income… broken promises. My husband decided that he would no longer wait on them to do what they promised they would do. He eventually went out and got not one job, not two jobs, but three jobs total to help take care of the bills that were coming into our house.

We struggled financially during this season in our lives. It was very challenging. I am happy to say this though. Nobody knew that we were having such a hard time financially. We never called and asked people to borrow money. We didn't put on this sob story about what was going on. Nobody knew. My husband and I had purposed in our heart that despite the deceitfulness, despite the manipulation, we were going to do what we had to do to make it work. My husband worked so many hours with these three jobs. He was adamant about taking care of his home which is what I so dearly loved about him.

The difference between me and my husband is that we came from two different home environments. Financially, I grew up blessed. We never had a need for anything. My father always blessed me with loads of money. I had new cars to drive before I even had a license. Clothes and shoes were in abundance. There was no lack. We weren't rich, but we were well taken care of. My husband, on the other hand, was the exact opposite. He never knew what it was like to have abundance. He grew up learning how to make do with what they had. He grew up knowing and understanding that every dollar counted. I, on the other hand, wasted money on whatever I wanted at that time. You see, he understood what to do during this season of barrenness, this time when the money was looking real funny. Myself, on the other hand, didn't know how to handle it. I cried thinking about how they manipulated us. I cried because I couldn't go and get my hair done, and I cried when I couldn't shop for clothes and shoes. I acted like a big, spoiled baby... I know. It wasn't often that I did this, but I did have my moments. I didn't grow up in this type of environment so it didn't sit too well with me. My husband was just awesome! During my times of weakness, I remember him holding me and telling me that we were going to be alright. He told me to just trust him. He let me know that he would work ten jobs to make sure that I was well taken care of. He would do what he could until he found that perfect job. What a man! Oh, how I still love him after all these years!

    One day, my husband made up in his mind that he would go into the military. This would certainly help our financial situation. He would do training, and once he got out we would move to another location and I could get a job teaching there. I thought that was a brilliant idea! I was excited, or should I say at least for the moment I was excited. I agreed and the next thing I knew was that he was sent off to do basic training. He would be gone for three months.

That was such a horrible time for me! I was alone in a place where I knew no one. Financially, we were in a mess. I had no friends, no family. All I could do was go to work and come home to an empty apartment. I eventually went into a state of depression. I couldn't talk to my husband that often because he was in training, so letters had to suffice. It was horrible. My husband on the other hand, realized that military was a bad choice. Deep down inside, he knew that wasn't the plan that God had for our lives. He immediately took action. He began to talk to his leaders about his decision. He told them about how he needed to come home to be with me, that I was depressed with no one there to help. I talked to them about how the military may not have been a good fit for him. Eventually, he was able to get out and come back home.

From that point on, we made up in our minds that we were going to do whatever we needed to do to get on the right track in every area of our lives… spiritually, mentally, physically, and financially. Our first step… start going back to church. One day, as I was leaving the school that I was working in, I passed by this church. I saw several people coming out of it, and I said to myself, "Hey, maybe that's a good church to try." I told my husband about it, and the next Sunday we were there. We enjoyed it so much that we eventually joined. My husband and I decided that if we were going to do this, we were going to give it 110 percent. We realized that tithing was a big part of being a Christian. We were already in a financial slump, but we made up in our minds to trust God and the principles that He gave us on giving. We were going to give a 10 percent tithe and offering no matter what our bank account looked like. We were willing to make the sacrifice and trust God.

When I say that God did a quick work; he absolutely did a QUICK work!! The next week after paying our tithes, my husband got a call from a bottling company to come and work for them full time. He would receive a very nice salary and bonuses to go along with it!! We were amazed at what God had done. Just like that, our finances had changed all because we chose to be obedient to the word and pay our tithes and offering!

It didn't end there. As we continued to pay our tithes and offering, within six months of almost every year that my husband worked for this company, he received a promotion. God had showed him so much favor that he eventually became the number two man on the job for that local plant. There was only one position above him. God is so good!

Eventually, my husband began to want more. He wanted to go to that next level. He chose not to be content with where he was at. He wanted to go higher. Well, there was only one catch. With there being only one person above him in that local company, the only way he could get that position was if this person resigned, transferred, got fired, or died. Well, it didn't seem like any of that was going to happen anytime soon, so the only option was to move. As I was growing more and more in the Lord, I began to seek his face. I asked Him about us moving. I will never forget that day. The Holy Spirit spoke to me and said, "This is where I planted you, and this is where you will grow." I then questioned God. I said, "Well Lord, if this is where you want us, then open up the door for my husband to get that position without us having to move." I would say two days later, my husband came to me with the most exciting news. He was excited about some company calling him about a position that would be the EXACT same position that he wanted with the current company that he was with. They would pay him the salary that he wanted, give him a company car, and he wouldn't even have to move!! But get this… he didn't even apply for the job!!! They just called him out of the blue about this position.

    I knew it was God. I shared with my husband the conversation that I had with the Lord a few days before. I let him know that God just simply answered my prayer. If we were not supposed to move, I simply asked him to open that door for my husband, and he did just that. God never seizes to amaze me!

    You see, this season of financial barrenness was truly a test for us in our marriage and in our spirit man. Many marriages today fall into the category of divorce all because of financial issues, or should I say, financial barrenness. As a matter of fact, it's one of the top reasons for divorce in today's society. So, how did we overcome it? We didn't let that interfere with our relationship. Before we had money, we had each other. I never belittled my husband. I never made him feel less of a man. I have always and will always continue to support him in everything that he does. He's my best friend. I love him more than I love money. We understood the importance of commitment, and loving each other in the midst of our financial chaos. When we couldn't do anything but eat Vienna sausages and crackers, we loved and enjoyed the quiet time that we had with each other. We chose to make each other the priority and not the money.

The next thing that we did was chose to develop a more intimate relationship with God together as a team, a married couple. We allowed Him to be the head, and not the tail, of our lives. We chose, as a family, to follow the financial principles of God in order for us to have financial success, which is still working today. We understood that if we put God and each other before our financial crisis, we would be alright. We did that and look at where we are today!

God has trusted us with even more money, and our very own businesses. Never allow where you are to dictate who you are. Yes, you may be in a land of barrenness when it comes to your finances, but know that it won't stop you from getting to your blessing. Yes, I wept during this time of my life because it did get hard; however, know that weeping may endure for a night, but joy cometh in the morning (Psalm 30:5). Stop focusing so much on your today. If you do, you won't even be able to see your tomorrow. You WILL come out of your financial barrenness sooner than you think. Sacrifice unto the Lord. Watch and see the blessings that He will pour unto you all because of your faith and obedience to Him. Trust God and see what happens!

CHAPTER 4

BARREN LAND # 2- INFERTILITY

Just the thought of having a child excited me! I knew that I had a special anointing to be a mother. After all, I did help my mom raise my brothers. I remember changing their diapers, singing them to sleep, feeding them their bottles, etc. I loved every minute of it! I knew that I would be the perfect mother for my own children one day, and I couldn't wait!

My husband and I were high school sweethearts. You might find this weird, but we loved each other since the first grade, before we even knew what love was all about. I remember clearly the day that my mom transferred me to his school. I was a bit nervous. I knew that I wouldn't know anybody, but I remembered him from my grandmother's because he lived in the same neighborhood with her. When he saw me, he would always try to play with me. He was always looking for me to come over to my grandmother's house so that he could come over and play or just hang out with us. At a very young age, there was a strong attraction that we simply couldn't avoid once we got in high school. It was in the latter part of our tenth grade year that we decided to start dating. We had made up in our minds that once and for all that we would stop flirting and make it official. How exciting!

Trish M

    A semester before I graduated from college, we ended up getting married after six years of dating. We were excited about our new move to Panama City, Fl. Upon moving, we had already discussed the idea of having kids. We decided to have our first child by the time we turned twenty-five years old. We wanted to enjoy our marriage first. We wanted to travel and see the world. It's funny how it all worked out. This was a really exciting time for us. We got a chance to do exactly what we said we would do. We traveled to eight different islands in the Caribbean. We traveled to several different vacation sites within the United States. We most certainly had a blast! We soon realized that twenty-five was coming upon us soon, and guess what? It was time to start working on that family!

    I was in for a rude awakening! We tried for almost a year with negative results. I soon began to research fertility specialists in the Panama City area. At that time, I found one whom we will just call Dr. F. Dr. F. seemed just as nice as he wanted to be. He was willing to help me and my husband accomplish our goal, our dream of becoming parents. After all, we were the perfect couple who had loved each other since the first grade, right? Who knew it would be this difficult to bring forth a child between two people as loving as us? Well, he told us what we needed to do to be successful. His first recommendation was to start me on Clomid, which is a fertility drug that is effective in stimulating ovulation. He diagnosed me with Polycystic Ovarian Syndrome. For those that don't know, Polycystic Ovarian Syndrome, or PCOS, is an endocrine disorder and a common cause of infertility in women. In PCOS, hormones that affect the reproductive system are abnormal, leading to irregular or absent ovulation. It is a common disorder, affecting up to eight percent of women. Women with this syndrome often have polycystic ovaries. This means that the ovaries have many tiny, benign and painless cysts. During an ultrasound exam, the tiny cysts may resemble a string of pearls (About.com- Rachel Gurevich). So, that was my label. That was my hindrance, my stronghold, the very thing that was keeping me from being a mom! I was determined to not let that hinder our vision!

We began the Clomid treatments with high hopes of positive results. I remember that we fasted and prayed a lot to God about this because we were not dependent upon the medicine, but we were dependent upon the grace of God to allow us to be successful. Month after month we took the medication with negative results. Finally, after about four to six months of trying, we decided to stop for a little while… we needed a break from it all. Within one month of us making this decision, we found out that we were pregnant. How excited we were to get this news! Just think, after months of trying with the medication and negative results, to get positive results without taking the medicine was what seemed to us like a miracle by itself!

I didn't want to stop looking at the pregnancy test. I couldn't believe that we were really seeing two lines! Oh my goodness… had this really happened? Of course we ended up taking several tests which all proved to be positive. We were excited to go to the doctor to get the same positive results that we got at home. We were so amazed that God had allowed this to happen!

Within a week of having those positive results, I felt as though something wasn't right. My body felt weird. My womb… something was going on that I couldn't explain. Another week passed, and I began to feel this tingling in my side. It wasn't really painful, but it did make me uncomfortable. Another week passed and it started to hurt a bit more. I also had spotting at the time. I went to the doctor to see what was going on. They did an ultrasound, and couldn't see a clear picture of the baby in the womb. Instead of getting concerned, Dr. F. simply told me that it was probably too soon to see anything, and to come back a few weeks later and they would check again. I started thinking, "Ok, well that just doesn't sound right." At that point in my life, I should have been about six weeks pregnant. Going into the seventh week, the pain in my side continued to grow more and more uncomfortable. I then called the doctor to complain about all the pain that I was going through. He asked me if I was bleeding. I told him that I wasn't bleeding, but I was still having some light spotting going on. His next question, "Is it red or is it brown?" I said, "It's brown." His response, "Well we really don't have to be concerned unless it's bright red and if you are having lower back problems." I then say, "Oh ok." But still, within me, I felt as though something wasn't right. No, I wasn't having lower back pains or bleeding, but my body felt as though something just wasn't right about it! I began to go online and research pregnancies that included pain in the side. I kept coming up with the same conclusion from all of my research… ECTOPIC PREGNANCY! Just the thought of it made me really nervous because I also read about women dying from that every single year. I began to pray even harder… "Father, I pray that my baby is in the womb. Lord, let everything be ok for me and for my child. Lord don't let anything be wrong. We prayed and fasted for this little one for so long. Father, please don't allow us to have a miscarriage!" That was a very common prayer during this time and season in my life.

The following week, week eight, the pain had gotten so unbearable that I couldn't even go to work. I took Tylenol for pain medicine. It did no good whatsoever. I called the doctor and explained what was going on. They told me to come in ASAP. I scheduled an appointment on that same day. Dr. F. did an ultrasound to see what was going on in my womb. Again, there was no clear picture of the baby. They took another pregnancy test, and it was still positive. Again, Dr. F. begins to say, "Maybe it's still too early to see anything." I began to question him. I asked him if this could be an ectopic pregnancy based on all my research and studies. He replied that it could be, but that he thought that it was just too early to see the baby on the ultrasound. He assigned me to bed rest, and told me to just kick my feet up.

Going into the ninth week of this pregnancy, the pain became so unbearable that I didn't know what to do. I called my doctor. They asked if I was bleeding yet, and I told them no. I was still only just spotting. They wanted me to continue to rest, and if it got any worse, I would just have to go to the emergency room. After I got off the phone, I began to pray really hard. I began to beg God to let this pain subside. I begged God to let my baby be okay. I pleaded with God to make this situation better for me. After I prayed, I began to feel better. The pain had subsided, and I was more-so just relaxing. My husband came home from work and asked me if I was feeling better. It was a miracle that the pain was gone, so I told him yes, I did feel better. But I also told him that even though I felt much better, deep down inside of me I felt that I still needed to go to the emergency room just to make sure that everything was okay since the pain that I had earlier was so intense. My husband agreed, and he helped me get ready to go to the hospital.

I had high hopes going into the hospital that everything was okay. I kept telling myself that the pain was gone now. I kept saying that the baby was okay. No need to worry. It is well. In the hospital, I began to tell them all of the issues that I was having. They immediately got me situated and began to do an ultrasound on me. This ultrasound in particular viewed my entire abdominal area instead of the womb. I can't begin to tell you how nervous I was looking at the screen. The technician wouldn't really answer any of my questions. She would only say that the doctor would review everything with me. Once she finished, the analysis was sent to the doctor. Within minutes of looking at the results, I had nurses and doctor running into my room. I had no clue what was going on. They began to explain to me that I had internal bleeding. They would have to do emergency surgery to stop the bleeding as quickly as they could. They also told me that the internal bleeding was coming from what they believed were my tubes rupturing from the "ectopic pregnancy," and they had a small amount of time to take the baby out and stop the internal bleeding. They let me know that there was a chance that, 1) I had lost my tubes and possibly never be able to have children, and 2) I could die from this. Wow, what in the world???? Ok, let's back up. First and foremost, they were telling me that this pregnancy is resulting in a miscarriage, that I was losing my child. Second, I might have lost my tube(s) because they could be ruptured. Third, not only have you lost a child, but your life could be lost at the same time if we don't hurry and do this emergency surgery! How much can someone take at one time? This was certainly devastating news! It was the grace of God that helped me to digest everything that they were saying to me. The only thing I could do was look at my husband, cry, and tell him to pray for me. I also told him that if I was not out of surgery by a certain time, that he needed to come and check on me. I was heartbroken. I was hurt. I was sick. I was frustrated. I didn't know what to do. I didn't know if I would live to see another day. I didn't know... I just didn't know. My heart was so heavy learning that my child was lost, and at the same time, my life could be lost as well. I couldn't even cry out! It was almost as if I was numb to everything they were telling me. Oh God, why have though forsaken me!!! I just cried as they rolled me to surgery.

    A few hours later, I woke up to find my husband by my side. Dr. F. was coming in through the door as he was the one that performed the emergency surgery on me. I saw him clearly walk through my door with a smile on his face and a manila envelope in his hands. He asked me how I was doing. I was speechless. I just shook my head as a tear rolled down my face. He began to talk about how much a success the surgery was. He was really excited that it went so well. Dr. F. began to explain to me that they performed the surgery just in the nick of time! They were able to save my tubes. They had not ruptured yet. They stopped the internal bleeding and were able to remove the baby with everything still in place. All I could see was the grin he had on his face from ear to ear. He then began to take pictures out of the manila folder showing me what the internal bleeding looked like. He showed me pictures of my fallopian tubes, pictures of the swollen tube with the baby. He was so proud of himself for performing his first successful ectopic pregnancy surgery! My life was saved even though the baby's life was lost. He grinned from ear to ear telling me how happy he was of the success, how happy he was that my tubes were saved, how happy he was that he stopped the bleeding as quickly as he did, and last but not least, how happy he was that it was such a success that my husband and I could try to have another baby. He started saying that once I healed from this surgery we were welcome to start back trying again.

As he was saying all of this to me, tears began to roll down my face. I couldn't believe that he was doing this. I had just lost my child. I didn't want to hear about how proud of himself he was for this being his "first" ectopic pregnancy surgery and how successful it was. It didn't excite me to see pictures of my tubes that enclosed a baby that I had just lost. It didn't excite me to hear him tell me that we could start trying again as soon as I healed from the surgery. It didn't excite me to see the internal bleeding that had taken place within my body. For crying out loud, I had just had a major surgery and lost a child at the same time! Where was the sensitivity? I was simply blown away. I couldn't tell him how I was feeling because I just… I just couldn't talk… I just… I couldn't express what I really wanted to say. I had been through so much that I didn't feel like talking to anyone. He left me with the pictures and the smile that he had on his face when he first appeared in my room. I couldn't do anything but weep as my husband held me close.

Not only was the entire surgery horrific, but the recovery from the surgery was even more horrible. Dr. F. put me on an eight week diet of only liquids. The only thing that I could eat was soup. Juice and water was fine. I couldn't even have crackers to go with my soup! What in the world???? My husband even tried to get creative with the soups by bringing in so many different varieties. It really didn't matter. My appetite was hardly even present on most days. It was so difficult to sit at home for six to eight weeks after going through what I had gone through. The surgery left me hurting so bad that I could hardly walk by myself. Not only that, I couldn't even take a bath by myself. My husband had to help me bathe. The only thing that I could really do was kick my feet up and stay in the bed. This was a BIG no-no! I couldn't go anywhere or do anything. I was left at home all by myself. The only thing that I could think of was all that I had gone through with this pregnancy. My heart was so broken. Words couldn't even describe the pain that I felt. My spirit was broken. We had prayed and fasted for so long and so hard for this child. To go through what we had just gone through… How do I describe it???? Ok, I'll give it my best shot. I thought about how I physically hurt throughout and how I was spiritually and emotionally hurting during this time. Spiritually, I couldn't pray for myself anymore. I had reached the lowest spiritual point of my life. I was so angry with God!!! Wait, let me change that. I was EXTREMELY angry with God!!!! I felt like he had loved others more than he loved me. I felt insignificant. I was seeing how he had blessed so many women with babies, so I began to wonder, "Why not me? What had I done so wrong?" There were women getting pregnant who weren't even trying, women all over the world getting pregnant who didn't even want to have a baby. I felt like God wasn't hearing my prayers because he was blessing everybody else except me and my husband. I began to tell God things like "Well, I won't be praying for myself anymore because it seems like you don't hear me. I'll just pray for everybody else because you seem to hear their prayers and bless them." I know this may seem childish in the eyes of many super-spiritual saints, but I have to be honest and tell you what I was feeling at that time. I was so angry at God that I didn't know what to do. I would cry myself to sleep from my emotional hurt. The emotional pain was just as hard as the physical pain. I began to think about all the seeds that I had sown. I had sponsored so many women's baby showers, decorated, prepared food, bought cakes, bought gifts etc. I even became a big time babysitter by watching everyone else's babies while they enjoyed evenings out with their spouses. I began to really enjoy sowing those seeds because I knew that one day, I would have kids of my own.

Did God even see that? Did he recognize how much I was blessing others? His word says that "you shall reap what you sow" (Galatians 6:7) So many times people use this text in a negative manner, but we are certain that it goes both ways… good and bad! Well, I had sown these "good" seeds, so I was "expecting" to receive a "good" harvest for my first pregnancy.

I felt like Jesus in the garden of Gethsemane when He was asking God if He had forsaken him. Why God? Why had you forsaken us in this critical time of our lives? Why couldn't this cup pass from us?

Nevertheless, God began to deal with my heart for a period of about six to eight months. When I would go to church, I felt numb on the inside. It was like I had no praise on the inside of me. It was like I had no joy. In this period or season of going through, God had sent some dynamic women of God to minister to me in order to help me get out of the rut that I was in. My pastor at that time would print out devotionals that I could read as well as kept me covered in prayer. She was truly a breath of fresh air that I really didn't want, but yet needed so badly. As I began to take those baby steps back to God, he began to reveal things to me. He began to show me how good He was to me in the midst of it all. He reminded me of the day that I decided to go to the hospital. He revealed it so clearly how I had prayed and asked Him to take the pain away, and how He did just that. Then, He revealed to me how it was his Holy Spirit that told me to go to the hospital even when the pain was gone away just like I prayed for it to do. He told me, "Daughter, when the pain had subsided and all seemed well, it was I who told you to go to the hospital anyway. It was I who allowed the timing to be perfect for them to stop the bleeding and save your tubes. It was I who allowed your tubes to still be in place. Daughter, it was I who put you in a situation to where you could still have children because I, by the functioning of my Holy Spirit, drew you to the hospital. Daughter, it was I!" Glory to God!!! He allowed me to see that if He hadn't told me to go to the hospital when I did, I could have lost my tubes as well as my life. It was by the glory of God that I shall live and not die!! Once I got that revelation, I had to repent and ask God to forgive me. I had to praise Him. I had to worship Him. I had to give Him thanks for what only he could do! I realized how selfish I was throughout this process. I was so stubborn and so prideful. I had to let the Lord know that I loved Him, and that I trusted Him no matter what. I was determined to be a mother, and I was not about to allow the enemy to stop it! We were ready to give it another try.

THE JOURNEY CONTINUES.......

As God dealt with my heart, I knew that no matter what, I was destined to be a mother. My husband and I continued on with the process of accomplishing just that. We began to seek the council of Dr. F. again. I must say, I was a bit hesitant because there was no way that he, Dr. F., should have let me go that far into the pregnancy without seeing that it was clearly an ectopic pregnancy! We pressed on and went with him anyway because after all, at that time, he was the ONLY fertility specialist in Panama City, which was really, really frustrating. Upon seeing Dr. F., he let us know the facts… that our chances of having another ectopic pregnancy was higher now. We understood that, but at the same time, we were trusting in God that this curse would never come upon us again! We were not going to let the FACTS interfere with the TRUTH… and that truth is that NOTHING is impossible with my God!

With that being said, Dr. F. then started us back on the Clomid. This time, we were successful a lot faster! I began to think to myself that God had redeemed the times, and He did it pretty quickly this time… wow! I can't begin to describe the feelings that we had… a bit nervous, excited, anxious, happy, ecstatic, etc.

Every since the first pregnancy, ultrasounds always made me extremely nervous! We never really got a chance to see our child on the screen like other parents who had a normal pregnancy. Going into the doctor's office for that ultrasound produced a great amount of fear on the inside of me. I didn't know what we would see. I kept telling myself to trust God. No matter what… trust God!

So, we go in for the ultrasound… nothing! Couldn't see ANYTHING in the womb! Dr. F. takes a pregnancy test... still positive. Next thing that I had to do was get blood work done to check the HCG levels. The results came in, and they were very low. I had already started miscarrying! A day or so later, the bleeding started, and I knew for sure that it was now over for this pregnancy.

I cried, cried, and cried some more. Again, I had the questions, "Why me? Why were we going through this yet again?" I began again to tell the Lord about how I didn't understand what was going on. We had failed again. This time, I didn't turn away from God. I let Him know that despite it all, I trusted Him. Whatever happened… I trusted Him.

It was hard getting over the second miscarriage as well. It wasn't as hard as the first time, but yet it was still very difficult. I don't think anything compares to the first miscarriage. It was much, much harder. This time, I went through the drought… I went through a depression, but I still moved forward trusting and believing in God. I was determined to not let the devil win this war!!!

THIRD TIME'S THE CHARM???

Speak positive. Think positive. Be positive in your attitude. These are things that I encouraged myself to do while trying to battle this war in my mind. On one hand, the enemy had me thinking that we would NEVER be able to have a child on our own. At one point, and for a very brief moment in our lives, we began to discuss adoption. The more I thought about it, the more it was confirmed in my spirit that it was NOT the route that my husband and I were to take. I mean nothing against adoption, but the Holy Spirit was confirming in my spirit even the more that we would bear our own children. I began to be hopeful again. It had been a year or so since my second miscarriage, and my husband and I were content with holding off.

After a year and a half or so, I began to have that urge to try again. Baby fever was upon me! My husband wasn't as eager as I was to start trying again because he said that he hated seeing me go through those depressive, disappointing moments. As much as he wanted a child, he wanted more for me to not go through all of that again. I assured him that I was stronger; that I was more prepared mentally; that I was ready. His ultimate desire was to see me happy, so eventually he agreed to give it another shot. On your mark… get set… go!!!! Wooooohoooooo!!!! I was very, very excited about this because

I knew that God was going to work all of this out for our good because we truly had a heart for God. We loved Him, and we trusted Him with our lives!

As we were preparing to start treatments again, we soon learned that Dr. F. had died of some medical condition. I must say that this truly saddened my heart because Dr. F. was such a sweet man, and he was someone who was very easy to get along with. What were we to do? All we knew was that we were ready to start again, and Dr. F. was the only specialist that we knew of. Oh, let the search begin again!

I began to ask friends and acquaintances about some of the local doctors around town who could help us out. We needed someone who specialized in fertility issues… no ifs, ands, or buts about it!

We found out about a doctor who we will call Dr. M1. Okay, so here we go. My first appointment with Dr. M1… let's just say that it was a bit surprising! As soon as I walked in the doctor's office, I noticed this older short man with glasses slowly walking to the nurse's station. He had on light blue scrubs. I began to think to myself... "Hum, that can't be the doctor because he seems rather old." After getting the information that he needed, he slowly walked back down the hall. Well, all I could think was that this was going to be an interesting visit.

It wasn't long before they called me to the back to see the doctor. I quickly learned that, yes, that little old man walking down the hall was indeed the doctor. He seemed to have many years behind him, but I must admit he was extremely nice and friendly; however, I needed someone that my family could grow with for many, many years to come. So, I decided that Dr. M1, who was extremely kind, just wasn't the doctor for my family. I began to ask around again and get thoughts and referrals from some of my friends at that time. Someone eventually recommended that I go to see Dr. M2 who was supposedly a good doctor. So, we decided… what the heck… it was worth a try, right?

At the onset, Dr. M2 seemed somewhat cool. No problems thus far. I made sure to explain my past history with him and everything that we had endured as a couple in regards to miscarriage. Dr. M2 went ahead and put us back on the Clomid prescription that we had before. Within a month of trying, we became pregnant again. Yippee!!! Okay wait… hold your horses because you know how this could go. As soon as I got a positive result, I immediately scheduled an appointment with the doctor. They sent me orders to get blood work done so they could have an idea of where my HCG levels were at by the time I came in for my appointment.

When I got to Dr. M2's office, I must say that my husband and I were very nervous though neither of us chose to admit it. In my mind, I kept thinking to myself... "Third time is the charm, right Lord?" I wanted this pregnancy to be the "one." Our spirits were in such high expectation that God would allow this one to work out for us. We just knew that He would!

When we went into the doctor's room, they asked me to get undressed from the waist down. They wanted to see if they could detect anything on the ultrasound. Okay, so… by now, my hands are sweating. Could this be it? That was the question that was ringing through my head.

Dr. M2 came in with an expressionless look on his face. It had taken him a minute to come in, but he finally made it. So now, he goes straight into the ultrasound… I hear crickets… Right about now, he says nothing. He continues to move the handle over my womb as if he was searching for something. Still says nothing. Okay, right now I really just want to scream!!!! Say something dude!!!! That's what I was thinking in my head. Eventually, he slowly says, "Well, I don't see anything on the screen to indicate this as being a successful pregnancy. Where is her lab work?" he says to the nurse who then begins to pull my file information out. He looks at it, and then he says, "Yeah, your numbers are really low, so this is most certainly a miscarriage," he says emotionless. At this time, I'm very tearful, and I have a lot of questions as this is now my third pregnancy that has resulted in yet another miscarriage.

I began to ask him questions on why this keeps happening. I wanted to know if it was something wrong with me medically as to why I kept miscarrying babies. I was very hurt, and at this point, I just wanted some answers. Dr. M2 who was still very emotionless, says to me "Who knows. Just keep trying, and eventually it will work out." At this point, I'm shocked! I'm speechless! All I could do is open my mouth with no words coming out, just tears of sadness strolling down my face. My husband knew how hurt I was, and he came over to hold my hand and hug my neck. Dr. M2 then says to me, "Well, I have to go. I got babies to deliver at the hospital." He then walks out the door with nothing else to be said. Total disbelief! How can a man be so rude, so careless, so emotionless, so… I nor my husband could really respond because we were still trying to take it all in. The nurse goes to get me some tissue to wipe my face, and by that time, I came out of my "shock mode," and I asked her how could he treat us like that? He knew our history. He knew that was our third miscarriage. How could he have been so uncaring? I didn't understand, but my husband let her know that we wouldn't be coming back to see them. The nurse understood our reasoning behind this and was in total agreement with us. She agreed that Dr. M2's behavior was totally unnecessary and very impersonal. I let her know that I would tell everyone that I could about his coldness toward us and that he was not the kind of doctor that came high on our referral list.

Hurt, distraught, insecure, low self esteem… Every negative feeling that one could think of … I'm sure that I was experiencing it at that moment in my life. This miscarriage wasn't as bad physically as the first or the second one that we had, but what made it almost intolerable was the response that we got from the doctor. I thought to myself… "Lord, can it get any worse?"

FORTH TRY... GRACE US LORD!

Trying to recover emotionally from the third miscarriage was very difficult. I kept thinking to myself about how uncaring Dr. M2 was toward us. It made me feel really, really sad... almost inadequate... mad, angry, frustrated... so many emotions continued to run through me. I prayed and asked God to lead us to a doctor who was compassionate and caring, and not only that, but someone who would help us to get to the bottom of ALL of these miscarriages.

Of course, my husband and I decided to take a little break to recover from our third miscarriage. First, we had to find a new doctor. We were both very adamant about not going back to see Dr. M2. He did NOT come highly recommended on our list to say the least.

As I was recovering mentally from the last miscarriage, I began to seek God even more on His purpose and plan for our lives. I knew that His word says to be fruitful and multiply, but it seemed that no matter how hard we tried, miscarriage seemed to find us. I really began to question God on whether or not it was meant for us to have children. I began to get confused again, second guessing myself because of all the heartache and pain we kept enduring. Nevertheless, I was determined not to give up. I had always felt in my heart that I was destined to be a mother no matter what the enemy had done. I knew that in my heart of hearts we were destined to be parents. I was destined to be somebody's mother, and I was adamant on not giving up on that dream! #Determined

One day, in which I remember like it was just yesterday, I had a supernatural vision. I remember it so clearly. I was dusting the furniture in my living room and cleaning the glass of the coffee table, when suddenly, inside of the glass, God showed me a vision of two newborn babies!! I saw them so clearly through the glass of the table. They were diagonal from each other. I couldn't believe what I saw, but I knew that it was a sign from God. I knew it was Him telling me to hold on, to not give up. I knew He was showing me what was to come. I immediately began to praise God. I knew that He cared enough about what we were going through that He showed us a vision, a sign from heaven. I couldn't wait to tell my husband about it! As soon as he got in from work, I told him all about the good news and what God had shown me on that day. I remember telling him, "Honey, I don't know if God was saying that we would have twins or if He was saying that we would have two children. All I know, is that we are going to have two children, whether they are twins or not!!!"

This vision gave me so much hope for our future. It put a burning fire within me to get to the promise that God had shown me. I was so happy that I didn't know what to do with myself. "God cares! He really, really cares about what we are going through!" I thought to myself. I just knew that after that particular vision, we couldn't help but be successful with our next pregnancy.

As time went on, we still had not found a new doctor to take the place of the HORRIBLE Dr. M2. Of course, we couldn't get back on the treatments without having a prescription. So, we carried on about our business as usual. I still didn't give up on the search for a new doctor. I was talking to one of my friends, and she told me that Dr. I. was a really, really good doctor. I agreed to give him a shot when that time came.

Then one day, I realized that I had not had a cycle for that particular month. "Hum," I thought. "Well, I can't be pregnant because we didn't have any treatments done." What was going on with my body? I had absolutely no clue whatsoever. Then, it dawned on me… go ahead and take a pregnancy test anyway.

Within a minute of taking the test, I saw two pink lines come up… "Oh my goodness… we're pregnant," I thought to myself. I began to think that this HAD to result in success because we didn't take anything to assist with the conception. "God truly has his hands on this," I thought to myself. Immediately, I began to think about Dr. I. and how I had to hurry and schedule an appointment with him to make sure everything was okay. So, I did. I was prepared to take the necessary steps. I just knew that this pregnancy was blessed of God. My spirit was expecting that this time… this was it. Now was our time… I claimed it in Jesus name!

Trish M

Before I had a chance to make it to Dr. I's office, I began to spot, and slowly my dreams of a successful pregnancy began to fade away again. I knew that this wasn't a good sign based on my history. At this point, I was almost numb to the thought that this was another miscarriage, number four to be exact. I went into Dr. I's office knowing that there was a great chance that he would tell me that this pregnancy was unsuccessful.

As Dr. I entered into the exam room, he entered with a smile that was soothing and comforting to the spirit. He was a middle age, Caucasian man… a little bit of grey hair, glasses, slightly tanned with a somewhat tall not quite muscular stature. He greeted me with a smile and a short introduction of himself. I immediately knew in my heart of hearts that I was in good hands.

We began to talk about why I was there and about my history with miscarriages. Dr. I. did a pregnancy test which came back positive. He then did a pelvic ultrasound to see if anything could be seen in the womb… again, nothing was there. The spotting had now turned red, and he concluded that yes, I was going through yet another miscarriage, which would make my forth one.

Dr. I. was very, very compassionate as he shared the news with us. He showed a great deal of concern for us, which was the exact opposite of what we had just experienced with Dr. M2. Dr. I. began to discuss possible reasons for the frequent and continuous miscarriages. He then ordered a specific set of blood work to be done, which in turn would help us to figure out the reasons behind the frequent miscarriages. He assured me that we would get to the bottom of it so that my husband and I could finally bring forth a healthy, beautiful baby. I felt assured. Dr. I. had given me hope which was exactly what I needed.

The next day, there was a service at my church where we would have a prophet come in by the name of Prophet Walker. I must admit, I was feeling a bit down in the dumps having just learned about our forth miscarriage. Spiritually, I was feeling pretty low. I remember asking God to speak a word through his vessel that would encourage me and my husband to not give up. After all, we WERE going through our forth miscarriage at that very moment.

The service was awesome. Prophet Walker pretty much prophesied the entire service! It seemed like he had gotten to everyone in the building except for… you guessed it… me and my husband. I began to tell myself that God just didn't have a word for us that night. Right before he got ready to close out, he beckoned for me to come to the front where he was at. Immediately, I began to think that God had NOT forgotten about us. I knew that I needed to hear from God, and I prayed that he would use Prophet Walker to speak a word of comfort and encouragement to us.

As my husband and I stood together at the altar, the man of God began to ask us if we desired to have children. Wow! Look at God! He knew exactly what we needed. My husband and I both said yes. He then began to prophesy that by this time next year, we would have a child, and the child that we would have would be greatly blessed of God. He stated it again… that child would be greatly blessed of God! I was excited, overwhelmed, speechless… so many emotions ran through me. The only thing that I could do was cry at the altar. I cried because I was so happy! I was so happy that God had decided that enough was enough! Remember, I was going through my forth miscarriage on that same day. So, I had to see past my mess of a situation, in order to see, hear, and believe that God was going to bless us despite what we were going through. At that very moment of going through, I chose to trust God. I chose to take Him at His word. I chose to not focus on my "today," so that I could see my "tomorrow"… my future… the promise of God. God had a blessing with our names on it, and we were ecstatic about it!

After leaving that church service, my husband and I knew that soon we would be parents. We were so excited that we began to talk about names. I reminded my husband that we had a list that we had started for names already. We could go back and look at it, and keep adding to the list if needed. I then began to tell my husband about the baby being "greatly blessed of God" sounded so familiar to me. It was like I had heard or seen that somewhere before. When we had gotten home, I went and pulled the name list out that we had pre-composed, and I soon saw that we had only two names on the list – one for a boy and one for a girl. The kicker was… both names had the exact same meaning… "Great blessing or gift from God"… wow! God is AMAZING! The names that we had prematurely chosen were prophetic names!! We were not supposed to add any other names to the list because God had already given them to us. What a miracle!

After getting over that particular miscarriage and receiving the prophetic word from God, within two months of that, God allowed us to conceive! Dr. I. had already had me do a series of tests to see what my issue was. He narrowed it down to perhaps being some type of clotting disorder. He recommended that with the next positive pregnancy test, that we take shots (Blood thinning shots) to ensure that there were no complications or problems. Dr. I. was simply awesome. He was so compassionate and caring, and he helped us get to the root of our problem. We were so excited to give this another shot. Fifth pregnancy = total success!

During this pregnancy, we took the shots as instructed. We were finally able to do an ultrasound and see our baby on the screen!!! How exciting this was!! Tears of joy strolled down my face. This was one of the most precious moments in our lives because as you know, in the past, nothing ever showed up on the ultrasound to confirm that, yes, we were actually pregnant. This time was so much different. God did a supernatural thing with this child! Oh, how blessed this baby shall be!

At thirty-eight weeks, I went on to deliver a seven pound, eleven ounce baby boy by the name of DaeShaun Tynell

Trish M

Morrissette. When I first held him in my arms, the words that came out of my mouth were, "You're so beautiful." I couldn't believe it. Our dreams had finally come true. All the hardships, the pain, the struggles, the disappointments… After five pregnancies equaling four miscarriages and one live birth, we had finally arrived!!!! Glory be to God!

CAN WE DO IT AGAIN?

Our son had been such a joy, but after two years, we decided that he needed a play mate. After all, I reminded my husband of the vision that God had shown me a few years ago. I knew that He was going to bless us with at least two babies. Also, because we got our breakthrough by having our first child, I really and truly felt that the curse of miscarriage was broken off of our lives. Boy, was I in for a surprise!

Before getting to our second child, God allowed us to suffer through two more miscarriages. They both happened very early on within four to six weeks of the pregnancy. Again, with both of these miscarriages, we were never able to see any developments in the womb as proof that they were successful. At this point, I was again very numb when I heard the word "miscarriage." It always hurt, but for some reason, I had become emotionless. It wasn't that I didn't care. I cared tremendously. I just didn't know how to receive this. I knew that if I just didn't give up, God would cause the manifestation to occur like He did before. I knew that if we didn't give up, the vision that God showed me a few years ago of those two babies would soon be our reality.

I remember the weekend very clearly. I had been going through some stressful events prior to that weekend, and my husband and I felt that it would be great for us to rent a cabin in the mountains in the state of Georgia. We invited one of my husband's best friends from childhood, and his wife, to come along with us. What a blast we had! It was one of the most relaxing times that I had had in years! My husband and I were able to unwind, relax and enjoy each other's company.

During that weekend, our daughter was conceived. It was one of the most beautiful times of our lives. I must say, we – my husband and I – had endured a lot prior to that weekend. It was so great to just get away and focus on what was most important, our love, marriage, and commitment to each other.

Three weeks later, we found out that we were pregnant! Because of the dynamics of that weekend, I knew that this was our "love child." This child was meant to be here. The fear of miscarriage did not succumb me. I knew without a doubt that God's hand was all over this pregnancy.

This pregnancy was uniquely and miraculously different than the first one. For one, we didn't take any fertility treatments like Clomid. Secondly, I didn't have to take shots every day of the pregnancy. The doctors suggested the intake of aspirin instead. How miraculous was that, and what a testimony on the goodness of God! Thirdly, upon our first doctor's visit, we not only saw the baby, but we also heard the heartbeat – a sign to us to let us know that God had approved this pregnancy for success, and the devil was NOT allowed to destroy it this time.

I remember giving birth to this beautiful baby girl of eight pounds, four ounces by the name of Daesha Sanaa Morrissette. I saw the complete manifestation of what God had shown me several years in a vision. It was now complete. The vision had now come to full manifestation. I was so grateful and thankful to God. Despite the process, He had given us two healthy, beautiful babies. Our barren land of infertility was now a part of our past. We endured a process that took complete faith and trust in God, and because of that, we were able to reap a harvest that only God could get the glory for. Oh, how GREAT is our God!

CHAPTER 5

BARREN LAND #3- SPIRITUAL

Another word for "spiritual barrenness" is fruitlessness when it comes to things of the spirit. It can be a result of spiritual complacency or indifference. How can we be awakened from this "spiritual slump?" There is definitely a need for revival where there is an outpouring of the spirit in order to produce a fruitful field that will yield bountiful crops. If you are living a life that is spiritually barren, then you are living a life that is lacking joy... it's almost like you are going through a wilderness – a place that is dry, desolate, and deserted... A place where you feel alone, where no one quite understands what you are going through.

    We are all humans, and we go through dry, desolate moments from time to time, but it is also very important for us to remember that God promised to give us an abundant life (John 10:10), and if we are living spiritually barren, then we are in a very bad situation. We have to make up in our minds that we will NOT stay in this place for long. We have to press our way through. This spiritual desert can even be a positive experience that brings you to a higher level of prayer. If you are determined to see your way out, then you've got to be ready to pray your way out!

With spiritual barrenness, many times the enemy will try to talk you out of praying because he wants you to stay in the state that you are in. The devil knows that with prayer comes power to overcome him and all his tricks and schemes. Other reasons for not praying your way out of spiritual barrenness outside of what the enemy is doing could come from any of the following causes:

1) Focusing on your problems instead of God
2) Expecting an instant solution or putting God on our timetable
3) Failure to get in your word daily
4) Failure to regularly attend church services and be encouraged by other believers
5) Un-confessed, un-repented sin in your life that you refuse to give up
6) Excessive busyness with your career, family, or personal life
7) Physical exhaustion, depression, or emotional burnout

Sometimes, you might need help from your pastor, another believer, or a family member to determine the cause of your spiritual barrenness. It may be one or several of the above reasons, or maybe it's something unique to you. A heartfelt request to God can reveal much. His light not only helps you understand the world, but also yourself.

If you are able to identify the cause, then you can start to work on the remedy. Asking God for his assistance is major.

God can bring us out of any mess that we get ourselves in. He reminds us in His word that we can do all things through Christ who strengthens us (Philippians 4:13). There is no mountain that's too big for us. We are able to tell that mountain to be removed and cast into the sea.

As I think back on my "spiritual barrenness," it all happened during the time of my first miscarriage that you read about in the last chapter. I went through this barrenness for a sum total of eight months. I remember it being extremely hard to come out of. It was so difficult. I found myself experiencing many of the seven causes that I previously listed above. I began to focus on my problem more than I focused on God. I knew that I was hurting physically, mentally, and emotionally.

That seemed to take over my thoughts of God and who He is and what He was actually capable of doing. Instead, I began to think about how God cared for other people more than He cared for me. I began to think that He didn't love me, that He didn't want to bless me. All I saw was so many other women out there popping babies out of their womb like it was nothing, but yet I was struggling, yet I miscarried…not one time, but six times… yet I almost died… All I could think was… "where is God? How could He let us go through this?" I began to focus on the problem more than I was focusing on God, not realizing that God was the all-sufficient God, the all-powerful God, the Omni-present God… I forgot that God was and is Jehovah

Jirah… our provider… I forgot that He was well able to meet me at my point of need. I was so consumed in thinking on my problems….that my problems became BIGGER than my God!

And then, I began wanting an instant solution from God. All I knew was that I wanted to have a baby, and I wanted to have it now! I needed God to move on my timetable and not His own. When He didn't, my spirit became vexed. I was greatly disturbed in my spirit man. Soon, this led me to not reading my word on a daily basis, not being able to feed my spirit like I should have. Instead, I became malnourished in the spirit realm, thus leaving the door wide open for a spiritual barrenness to come upon me. You could see me in the natural and I would look healthy, beautiful, and strong, but, oh my,… to see me with your spiritual eyes would have been a different story. Not only did I lose the desire to get in my word, but I also lost the desire for praise, for worship, for even being in the house of God. Why? Because my problem became so much BIGGER than my God. It was like… nobody would understand… not even God Himself. It was like… who could help me? Who could help us? If God didn't do it and wasn't doing it, then who could? I felt alone in my barrenness. I felt misunderstood. I felt like I was being punished. I soon fell into a state of depression. I was at home every day for eight weeks, and all I could do was look at the walls. I decided to stop praying about my situation because God wasn't listening. He wasn't paying attention to me anymore. What was I to do?

How did I get out of this "spiritual rut?" How did I leave this spiritual barrenness… this spiritual desert? It was hard, but eventually I made up in my mind to not give up on God. He never gave up on me, so why should I do Him like that? I began to pray again. I began to hope again. I began to dream again. I felt myself getting closer and closer to God. I let the Lord know that I was willing to trust Him again. I repented for the way that I was acting. I realized that I walked in a spirit of pride… this spirit keeps you focused on EVERYTHING being all about… you guessed it… self! I was so concerned about me, me, me… that I couldn't see or think about anything else.

I fought my way out of it. As I was preparing to give you some steps to overcoming this, I ran across this article that said everything that I wanted to say. Check out these steps for overcoming spiritual barrenness by Liz Mason, creator of the Let's Get It Together Empowerment System:

OVERCOMING SPIRITUAL BARRENNESS

18Early in the morning, as he was on his way back to the city, he was hungry. 19Seeing a fig tree by the road, he went up to it but found nothing on it except leaves. Then he said to it, "May you never bear fruit again!" Immediately the tree withered. Matthew 21:18, 19 (NIV)

Going through the motions each day you make a plea to do well and be protected. You say a few words as you rush about your day. Never really taking time to look inside for whatever God wanted to change. Hurried out the door you think tomorrow is when I'll do things differently; tomorrow I'll make that much-needed adjustment in my schedule. You insist, God understands and you're right. He knows all about the reasons why you've decided to go about your day this way. You're just too busy, right? On the outside your leaves are green and things appear to be growing, but underneath the lush green foliage there isn't any fruit.

What happened to the fruit that you were meant to bear? Did your life become so busy that you simply failed to stay connected? No one needs to tell you whether your life is fruitful or not. Consider your ways, your thoughts and your time. No one needs to help with this one; you know the truth. Take time now to examine your results. If you are surfing through life doing what looks right, but on the inside you're spiritually dying, then be honest with yourself, and face the hidden truth that your life isn't bearing much fruit. Jesus was hungry and went over to check the fig tree for figs. It looked good from afar, but under closer examination it was clear that no fruit existed. Fruitlessness is a state that many Christians easily fall into, but it's completely avoidable.

Your life is meant to bear much fruit; good, healthy produce that supplies nutritional value to others. When you are in Christ, your life produces fruit, and that fruit endures. Without Christ you run the risk of never producing anything of value. **"Yes, I am the vine; you are the branches. Those who remain in me, and I in them, will produce much fruit. For apart from me you can do nothing. John 15:5** (NLT)

Barrenness creates an urgent need for God's help. If you look at your life and realize things just aren't what they should be, don't make the common mistake of trying to fix it on your own. Ask God for help. He will guide you and give the strength to make the much-needed change. Approach His throne with boldness. **Let us then approach the throne of grace with confidence, so that we may receive mercy and find grace to help us in our time of need. Hebrews 4:16** (NIV) All the answers you need to live a more balanced and productive life are found there. God wants you to have huge success; slow down long enough to ask Him for His help. Not just another quick and shallow, "Lord help me today," but really seek to know His ways. Reach out to God and seek to live your life the <u>specific</u> way He desires. Tarry until you push beyond your flesh (what you want and how you feel) and experience the long-awaited breakthrough.

Allow God to cut back the extra foliage. Let him cut away the unfruitful things so that your life (and the body of Christ) will be more productive. **He cuts off every branch of mine that doesn't produce fruit, and he prunes the branches that do bear fruit so they will produce even more. John 15:2** (NLT) What a difference you'll begin to experience as He prunes you and frees you from anything that slows your growth.

CHAPTER 6

NEW LEVEL OF FAITH

I've learned that as we are being challenged with difficulties in life, we must also challenge our faith as we go through the trials and the tribulations. In the midst of going through, we have to go on through so that we can get to the other side where our breakthrough lies. We must psych our minds to know and believe that we really can make it; that we can achieve whatever it is that we are believing God for. Though we don't see it, we have to trust God for the things hoped for and the things that we are not able to see with our very own eyes. We have to believe without a shadow of a doubt that though we don't see it (no sign of manifestation in the natural), God is yet doing it… whether it's seen or unseen, known or unknown… God is still yet doing it. We have to know that we serve the God of the impossible, that nothing is too hard for him to accomplish.

So, what's next? You have to be ready for a new level of faith. What do I mean by "new level?" New level means a new extent, a degree of intensity, an achievement or measure according to dictionary.com's definition. The word of the Lord declares that EVERY man is given a "measure of faith." Whatever your level is, work on going to that next level; work on getting to another degree or another level of intensity—let your faith be as intense as your trials and tribulations. Allow them to feed off of each other, and do your best to let your faith be bigger than your drama, bigger than your trials, bigger than your situation! The word of the Lord says that even a mustard seed faith has the power to move mountains. So, even with that small of a faith, you can do great things, but I have to challenge you. Are you content with mustard seed faith, or are you ready and willing to go to another level of faith? You see, if mustard seed faith can move a mountain, just imagine what your faith will do if it's bigger than a mustard seed. My, oh my!

Of course, the enemy doesn't want to see you go to the next level in your faith. He would rather you struggle and be hopeless at the same time. He would rather you cry over yourself and your life; things that you don't have, things that you lack, things that are happening to you… he wants you to become depressed, to feel like you just can't make it, to feel like nobody loves or cares for you… to feel like you are defeated… as if you just can't win! He would rather that you cry than speak forth the word of the Lord… speaking faithfully into the atmosphere, declaring that by faith, God is going to meet every need; by faith, there shall be no lack but abundance; by faith, you shall live and not die! You see, the enemy would rather you waddle in your mess than to see you stand firm on the word of God. You see when you're going through, it seems much easier to feel sorry for yourself rather than to stand firm and faithfully on what you are believing God to do. Well, I got news for you. There is HOPE! You don't have to be stuck, stagnant, or even stripped of what God has for you. Encourage yourself in this faith walk to not give up, and to not give in. I want to share with you some ways of accomplishing this.

1) Be mindful that the word of God tells us something very specific. "**Do not be anxious about anything,** but in every situation, by prayer and petition, with thanksgiving, present your requests to God" (Philippians 4:6 NIV). Go to God in prayer. **Pray simply and honestly about how you feel and what you are going through as much as you need to.** This will not only strengthen your faith but will ease your stress as well. God doesn't mind you being real and transparent with him. Remember, He is the God that sees all and knows all. He tells us to cast our anxieties (cares) upon him because He cares for us (1 Peter 5:7 NIV). God wants to know all about your problems, your troubles, trials, and tribulations. He really does care. *Don't be so caught up in being anxious about whatever it is that you have going on that you can't even pray to God.* All you are concerned about is what you don't have, what's being done to you, what you need, etc. God tells us in his word that man should not live by bread alone (Luke 4:4 NIV). We have to realize that life is so much more than whatever it is that we are anxious for. We just have to trust God's word and believe that we can actually have it.

2) **<u>Find you a scripture that speaks to your situation and memorize it.</u>** Begin to speak that same scripture or scriptures when you start to feel down or depressed, when you start to doubt whether or not God can do it, when you start to fear that it can be accomplished. Believe in God's love for you and that He will not lie to you. Some promises you can recite are: Philippians 4:13 NIV "I can do all things through Him who gives me strength" and Philippians 4:19 NIV *"And my God shall meet all your needs according to His riches in glory in Christ Jesus"* and Romans 5:3-5 NIV *"3 Not only so, but we also glory in our sufferings, because we know that suffering produces perseverance; 4 perseverance, character; and character, hope. 5 And hope does not put us to shame, because God's love has been poured out into our hearts through the Holy Spirit, who has been given to us."* It is so important to persevere and not give up on God or your situation. See, when we hope in man, man tends to fail us from time to time, but God... He NEVER fails us. He's an on time God. So make sure to put His word to work in your life so that you can build up your faith and your confidence in the Lord.

3) Okay, so... this one is the kicker. Often times, when we are going through something and our faith is being challenged, we tend to not want to hang around people. We put ourselves in this box, and we don't want to come

out of it until WE decide to come out of it. See, it's in that box where you find security because it's almost like it hides your troubles and your pains from everyone else. You don't allow them to come in your box unless you want them to, and you already know that the box is only so big, so everybody can't come in. Many times, it's just you inside that box, and if the truth be told, that's exactly the way you want it during this season of your life. Well, I came to shatter that illusion! **<u>To get to a new level of faith, you HAVE to surround yourself with positive people.</u>** Surround yourself with good positive friends who will pray for you, encourage you and let you know their testimony and how they have made it through all the bad times in their life. Because if you don't, all you'll begin to think is "woe is me." All you'll begin to do is dig a deeper hole than you are already in, and put yourself in a smaller box so that you can close yourself off even more from the world so that there is barely any room for you let alone anyone else that tries to come in. I came to tell you that this is not the way to handle it. Instead of a new level of faith, you'll lead yourself to a new level of depression, anxiety, and fear. Get out of that box! Welcome sincere people into your life that will help motivate and encourage you to get out of the rut that you are in. Don't waste your time feeling sorry for yourself. It's so not worth it!

4) **<u>Write the vision and make it plain.</u>** What is it that you are so worried or concerned about? What is it that is bothering you? What is it that has you so consumed that now you're not yourself? Now you are no longer happy, but actually pretty weary. Now your smile is gone, and if you do smile, then more than likely it's "fake". Because it's fake, now you are wearing a mask so that people can't see the real you, people can't know what's really wrong in your life. I tell you, whatever it is that has you in this position, write it down. Write your situation at hand down, and then write down what you want the outcome to be. God has control of everything. He knows how much you can bear, what you need, and when you need it. You have to let go of any worries or concerns. Write things down that you are concerned about and pray for God to give you faith over the situation to believe that He can actually move that mountain of a problem out of your way. If you know that there is a small part of you that walks in doubt and disbelief that it can be worked out, then talk to God about it. When you write down your vision of how you want things to be, you are calling those things that are not as though they were. It doesn't matter what is… your finances, job, children, family, health, sickness, disease, depression, anxieties, marriage, etc. It doesn't hurt to write it down and to speak it in the atmosphere. What can you lose by doing that?

Absolutely nothing! But, you are showing obedience to God's word, and as we all know, obedience is better than sacrifice. Watch and see what God will do for you just off of obedience. And this, my dear, will certainly help take your faith to that next level.

5) **<u>Last, but certainly not least, READ, READ, READ!!! Read God's word daily….</u>** *"Consequently, faith comes from hearing the message, and the message is heard through the word about Christ",* Romans 10:17 NIV. Reading your word will help take your faith to another level like never before seen! Most people would love to have more faith. Even the disciples desired this (Luke 17:5). One of the major ways for us to grow our faith is through time in the Word or time with the Word in us. Our faith will never grow sufficiently through personal study alone. This context refers to the proclaimed Word (Romans 10:13-17). If we are to grow our faith we must spend adequate time in the Word personally and hearing it proclaimed! When we read God's word, it results in answered prayer. Jesus said that if we would continue in a vital relationship with Him and His Word remained in us, we could ask for whatever we wanted and it would be granted. Now, if we consider that His Word is in us, we must conclude that we would be praying in accord or consistent with His word and will (1 John 5:14-15 NIV). On the other hand, the wise man wrote that whoever

turned their ear away from hearing His Word, their prayer would be an abomination to God (Proverbs 28:9). I challenge you that whatever "slump" you are in, whatever "barren land" you are going through, take your faith to the next level by reading, studying, and knowing your word. Be able to declare and decree that "it is well" in the midst of it all, and believe that it is so!

SCRIPTURES TO STRENGTHEN YOUR FAITH

Quotes from the Living Bible

1 Peter 5:7

Let Him have all your worries and cares, for He is always thinking about you and watching everything that concerns you.

John 14:27

I am leaving you with a gift – peace of mind and heart! And the peace I give isn't fragile like the peace the world gives. So don't be troubled or afraid.

Philippians 4:6-7

Don't worry about anything; instead, pray about everything; tell God your needs, and don't forget to thank Him for His answers. If you do this, you will experience God's peace, which is far more wonderful than the human mind can understand. His peace will keep your thoughts and your hearts quiet and at rest as you trust in Christ.

Trish M

Psalms 40:1-3

I waited patiently for God to help me; then He listened and heard my cry. He lifted me out of the pit of despair, out from the bog and the mire, and set my feet on a hard, firm path and steadied me as I walked along. He has given me a new song to sing, of praises to our God. Now many will hear of the glorious things He did for me, and stand in awe before the Lord, and put their trust in Him.

Psalms 34:17-19

Yes, the Lord hears the good man when he calls to Him for help, and saves him out of all his troubles. The Lord is close to those whose heart is breaking; He rescues those who are humbly sorry for their sins. The good man does not escape all troubles – he has them, too. But the Lord helps him in each and every one.

Isaiah 40:31

Those who hope in the Lord will renew their strength. They will soar on wings like eagles; they will run and not grow weary, they will walk and not be faint.

Faith In A Barren Land

John 14:1-3

Let not your heart be troubled. You are trusting God, now trust in Me. There are many homes up there where my Father lives, and I am going to prepare them for your coming. When everything is ready, then I will come and get you, so you can always be with Me where I am. If this weren't so, I would tell you plainly.

Deuteronomy 31:6

Be strong! Be courageous! Do not be afraid of them! For the Lord your God will be with you. He will neither fail you nor forsake you.

Isaiah 41:10

Fear not, for I am with you. Do not be dismayed. I am your God. I will strengthen you; I will help you; I will uphold you with My victorious right hand.

Psalms 112:6-8

Such a man will not be overthrown by evil circumstances. God's constant care of him will make a deep impression on all who see it. He does not fear bad news, nor live in dread of what may happen.

Trish M

For he is settled in his mind that Jehovah will take care of him. That is why he is not afraid, but can calmly face his foes.

Psalms 32:7-9

You are my hiding place from every storm of life; You even keep me from getting into trouble! You surround me with songs of victory. I will instruct you (says the Lord) and guide you along the best pathway for your life; I will advise you and watch your progress. Don't be like a senseless horse or mule that has to have a bit in its mouth to keep it in line!

Hebrews 10:35-38

Do not let this happy trust in the Lord die away, no matter what happens. Remember your reward! You need to keep on patiently doing God's will if you want Him to do for you all that He has promised. His coming will not be delayed much longer. And those whose faith has made them good in God's sight must live by faith, trusting Him in everything. Otherwise, if they shrink back, God will have no pleasure in them.

Isaiah 26:3-4

He will keep in perfect peace all those who trust in Him, whose thoughts turn often to the Lord! Trust in the Lord always, for in the Lord, Jehovah, is your everlasting strength.

Psalms 37:7

Rest in the Lord; wait patiently for Him to act. Don't be envious of evil men who prosper.

James 5:7-8

Now as for you, dear brothers who are waiting for the Lord's return, be patient, like a farmer who waits until the autumn for his precious harvest to ripen. Yes, be patient. And take courage, for the coming of the Lord is near.

Romans 8:31-32

What can we ever say to such wonderful things as these? If God is on our side, who can ever be against us? Since He did not spare even His own Son for us but gave Him up for us all, won't He also surely give us everything else?

Trish M

Isaiah 41:13-14

I am holding you by your right hand - I, the Lord your God - and I say to you, don't be afraid; I am here to help you. Despised though you are, fear not, Oh Israel; for I will help you. I am the Lord, your Redeemer; I am the Holy One of Israel.

Hebrews 13:5-7

Stay away from the love of money; be satisfied with what you have. For God has said, "I will never, never fail you nor forsake you." That is why we can say without any doubt or fear, "The Lord is my Helper and I am not afraid of anything that mere man can do to me." Remember your leaders who have taught you the Word of God. Think of all the good that has come from their lives, and try to trust the Lord as they do.

Psalms 4:8

I will lie down in peace and sleep, for though I am alone, Oh Lord, you will keep me safe.

Isaiah 54:10

For the mountains may depart and the hills disappear, but My kindness shall not leave you. My promise of peace for you will never be broken, says the Lord Who has mercy upon you.

John 14:18

No, I will not abandon you or leave you as orphans in the storm – I will come to you.

Proverbs 3:5-6

Trust the Lord completely; don't ever trust yourself. In everything you do, put God first, and He will direct you and crown your efforts with success.

Philippians 4:11-13

Not that I was ever in need, for I have learned how to get along happily whether I have much or little. I know how to live on almost nothing or with everything. I have learned the secret of contentment in every situation, whether it be a full stomach or hunger, plenty, or want; for I can do everything God asks me to with the help of Christ Who gives me the strength and power.

Trish M

Psalms 37:8-11

Stop your anger! Turn off your wrath. Don't fret and worry - it only leads to harm. For the wicked shall be destroyed, but those who trust the Lord shall be given every blessing. Only a little while and the wicked shall disappear. You will look for them in vain. But all who humble themselves before the Lord shall be given every blessing, and shall have wonderful peace.

---

2 Chronicles 20:17

But you will not need to fight! Take your places; stand quietly and see the incredible rescue operation God will perform for you, Oh people of Judah and Jerusalem! Don't be afraid or discouraged! Go out there tomorrow, for the Lord is with you!

Romans 8:24-25

We are saved by trusting. And trusting means looking forward to getting something we don't yet have – for a man who already has something doesn't need to hope and trust that he will get it. But if we must keep trusting God for something that hasn't happened yet, it teaches us to wait patiently and confidently.

Romans 8:28

And we know that all that happens to us is working for our good if we love God and are fitting into His plans.

James 1:2-4

Dear brothers, is your life full of difficulties and temptations? Then be happy, for when the way is rough, your patience has a chance to grow. So let it grow, and don't try to squirm out of your problems. For when your patience is finally in full bloom, then you will be ready for anything; strong in character, full and complete.

Habakkuk 2:1, 3

I will climb my watchtower now, and wait to see what answer God will give to my complaint.

But these things I plan won't happen right away. Slowly, steadily, surely, the time approaches when the vision will be fulfilled. If it seems slow, do not despair, for these things will surely come to pass. Just be patient! They will not be overdue a single day!

CHAPTER 7

OVERCOMING IT ALL

I am an overcomer! I choose to overcome! Quitting is NOT an option, and I choose for it to NOT be in my vocabulary! Often times, it's so easy when the going gets rough, to just let it go; to give up and to give in when things just aren't going our way. Many times, we may think, "well, on to the next thing since this one didn't work". We don't realize that the very thing that we choose to give up on could be the very thing that God wants us to get through and overcome so that we can get to that next level of blessings and breakthroughs. I often time say that we live in a world where we as the body of Christ want a microwave blessing; we put it in, and within a matter of minutes it's ready. We don't want to go through the God ordained process that could include difficulties, loss, heart ache, frustration, and sometimes even pain. We fail to realize that our very own trials and tribulations of life are not for us. It's to help somebody else. We are to open up our mouths and share what God has done for us, how he brought us out, how we made it… so that the next man or woman can get the help and encouragement that they need.

As you have read, there are many different forms of common barren lands such as financial, fertility, and spiritual, but now,

I would love to discuss how to overcome them ALL! **To overcome them all, you must first have the mindset that you are an overcomer; that you can do EVERYTHING that you set your mind to do; that nothing is impossible for you because nothing is impossible with God and you are His child!** So, first… change your mind on how you see yourself, see your life, see your future… because it's only then that you can see your breakthrough.

So now, ask yourself, "do I have what it takes to overcome"? There is no question that adversity and setbacks will come in life. How you handle them makes all the difference between success and failure. When complications, obstacles or unexpected circumstances appear to block your path, you must be equipped with resourcefulness and perseverance to solve each problem. Being determined to find a way over, under, around or through the obstacle requires perseverance! It requires you to NOT give up, to not give in. You can move mountains one truckload at a time if your level of resolve remains strong. You have to understand that you are not going to find meaning in your life from the challenges, but you will find meaning in your life when you overcome those challenges. So again, ask yourself… "Do I have what it takes?"

Even though perseverance can pay off, most people are still not as successful as they could be because they fail to utilize one additional critical key in becoming a successful overcomer—God's help and backing. On our own, even with extraordinary effort, we do not have everything it takes to learn from and master the challenges of life (*John 15:4-5 Abide in me, and I in you. As the branch cannot bear fruit of itself, except it abide in the vine; no more can ye, except ye abide in me. I am the vine, ye are the branches: He that abideth in me, and I in him, the same bringeth forth much fruit: for without me ye can do nothing*).

You have to understand that you are more than capable, but until you realize that you need the help of the Holy Spirit, it's as though all of your efforts are null and void. In all of my going through, I had to consistently depend on God to help me each and every step of the way. The scripture Luke 1:37 stayed in my spirit, and I would tell myself constantly that NOTHING is impossible with my God. I knew that if I was going to overcome, I had to realize that no obstacle or situation was too hard for my God to handle… key words… MY GOD… I had to understand that God was the source of me overcoming any and everything that came my way, because if it was up to me alone, I would have given up a long time ago, but I knew that it was the Holy Spirit of God living within me that was empowering me to continue to move forward and to trust God no matter what it looked liked. Any one person trying to exist without Jesus Christ in their lives is missing the most practical and valuable asset available. God's help and backing produces major physical, mental, financial and spiritual dividends. You have to understand that FAITH is the currency to His kingdom and to you getting through any obstacle. So, how about you cash in some of your faith tokens?

Faith is the very thing that is going to cause God to move on your behalf. The word of God tells us that those that come to God must first know that He is God… and that He is a rewarder of those who diligently seek him (Hebrews 11). We must NEVER underestimate what God is capable of doing!

You must understand that having faith is a necessity, but you must also have personal effort to back that faith up. Many times, we as the body of Christ love to declare how we are waiting on God to do things in our lives. Well I beg to differ! You're not waiting on God, God is waiting on you! He tells us that he has given us ACCESS to every spiritual blessing in heavenly places (Ephesians 1:3). God has given us the ability to gain wealth, the ability to overcome, the ability to be prosperous… the ability to do WHATEVER it is that we set our minds to do. The power to overcome is within us. We first have to believe and then walk it out by faith. We have to actively work to overcome obstacles and trials with persistent effort. God expects us to do our part. He wants each of us to use and develop the mind and ability that He has given us, and that requires firsthand experience. We need to work like the solution depends on us while relying on God to direct our paths (*Psalm 32:8 I will instruct thee and teach thee in the way which thou shalt go: I will guide thee with mine eye*). This provides the added security and powerful backing only our Creator can provide. Active living faith produces effort and work (*James 2:18-20 [18] Yea, a man may say, Thou hast faith, and I have works: shew me thy faith without thy works, and I will shew thee my faith by my works. [19] Thou believest that there is one God; thou doest well: the devils also believe, and tremble. [20] But wilt thou know, O vain man, that faith without works is dead?*). In order to truly overcome any situation, you must decide once and for all that you WILL have faith WITH works. You step forward believing and trusting God the entire way through, no matter what your situation looks like. We have to understand that it is our faith that is going to move God to act on our behalf. Again, faith is the currency of the kingdom. Don't you think that it is high time that you cashed in some of your faith tokens?

Imagine this. What if, in the midst of you going through your trial, tribulation, or situation… what if you could hear the still small voice of the Holy Spirit whispering in your ear…*"Do not fear; do not give up; know that I am with you always. You can do this. I have equipped you to be an overcomer."* Would you keep pressing? Would it be easier for you to not give up? If you could constantly hear your own personal cheerleader, the Holy Spirit, tell you that you are an overcomer, would you believe Him? Again, the first step to overcoming any situation in life is believing that you can do it. Once you make up in your mind to believe, you have to walk by faith and not by sight. If you focused on what you see with your eyes and not what you see with your faith, then you are more prone to give up. But if you see with your faith, then you just opened up a door called "breakthrough" to manifest in your life.

Even though we want a "breakthrough," there will be times when there is nothing we can do to solve a problem or overcome an obstacle. Often when circumstances are beyond our control, it is more difficult to persevere. But when we humbly wait on God and submit our will to His, we grow in faith and character. God may choose to simply work out circumstances to solve the problem, or He may allow the problem to persist to perfect our faith and increase our reliance on Him (*2 Corinthians 12:8-10 [8] For this thing I besought the Lord thrice, that it might depart from me.[9] And he said unto me, My grace is sufficient for thee: for my strength is made perfect in weakness. Most gladly therefore will I rather glory in my infirmities, that the power of Christ may rest upon me.[10] Therefore I take pleasure in infirmities, in reproaches, in necessities, in persecutions, in distresses for Christ's sake: for when I am weak, then am I strong.*) Regardless, of what it is that we are going through, we must persevere to the end (*Romans 5:3-5 ³ Not only so, but we[c] also glory in our sufferings, because we know that suffering produces perseverance; ⁴ perseverance, character; and character, hope. ⁵ And hope does not put us to shame, because God's love has been poured out into our hearts through the Holy Spirit, who has been given to us.*)

If we allow God to get involved in our lives, situations, opportunities and even trials will have deeper and more purposeful meaning. God places our spiritual growth ahead of our physical comfort and success. So should we. (*James 1:2-4 Consider it pure joy, my brothers, whenever you face trials of many kinds, because you know that the testing of your faith develops perseverance. Perseverance must finish its work so that you may be mature and complete, not lacking anything*)

When we humbly wait on God and submit our will to His, we grow in faith and character. When we persevere though trials and circumstances—which God allows for our good—godly character can develop. (*Hebrews 12:11 Now no chastening for the present seemeth to be joyous, but grievous: nevertheless afterward it yieldeth the peaceable fruit of righteousness unto them which are exercised thereby*).

Overcoming trials can produce the character God wants. At the same time, we can be comforted in knowing that God will provide a way out of them. (*1 Corinthians 10:13 There hath no temptation taken you but such as is common to man: but God is faithful, who will not suffer you to be tempted above that ye are able; but will with the temptation also make a way to escape, that ye may be able to bear it*).

In summary, overcoming obstacles is not something that is impossible. You must have a made up mind. You must know that you know. You must have a "make it happen" mindset that you can do anything that you set your mind to do. No matter what your barren land is, you must first know that nothing is too hard for you because nothing is too hard for your God. You serve the God of the impossible. He MAKES the impossible possible. He MAKES the crooked places straight. He's the God that split the sea and caused Moses to walk on dry land. He's the God that turned water into wine. He's the God that healed the sick, raised the dead, fed thousands with a few fish and five loaves… know that no matter what your situation is, God is well able to bring you out. In order to overcome, you must be willing to follow these simple steps:

1) Believe in yourself
2) Activate your faith
3) Seek God to assist you
4) Figure out steps that will lead you to a positive direction
5) Surround yourself with positive people
6) Stay focused
7) Encourage yourself. The power of life and death is in your tongue, so open up your mouth and speak into the atmosphere calling those things that are not as though they were.
8) Don't quit

If you choose not to give up, if you choose to trust God, if you choose not to give in… then God has a blessing and a breakthrough with YOUR name on it!

Inspirational Quotes For Being an Overcomer

"Wanting something is not enough. You must hunger for it. Your motivation must be absolutely compelling in order to overcome the obstacles that will invariably come your way."
~Les Brown~

"Courage doesn't always roar. Sometimes courage is the quiet voice at the end of the day saying, "I will try again tomorrow."
~Mary Anne Radmacher~

"You gain strength, courage, and confidence by every experience in which you really stop to look fear in the face. You are able to say to yourself, "I have lived through this horror. I can take the next thing that comes along." . . . You must do the thing you think you cannot do."
~Eleanor Roosevelt~

"The most important thing in the Olympic Games is not to win but to take part, just as the most important thing in life is not the triumph but the struggle. The essential thing is not to have conquered but to have fought well."
~unknown~

"If you are not criticized, you may not be doing much."
~Donald H. Rumsfeld~

"Obstacles don't have to stop you. If you run into a wall, don't turn around and give up. Figure out how to climb it, go through it, or work around it."
~Michael Jordan~

"You're on the road to success when you realize that failure is only a detour."
~Anonymous~

"Our greatest glory is not in never falling, but in getting up every time we do."
~Confucius~

"When you climb to the top of the obstacle that is blocking your view, you are able to look at your situation from a different perspective."
~Lucy MacDonald~

"Yesterday I dared to struggle. Today I dare to win."
~Bernadette Devlin~

www.ingramcontent.com/pod-product-compliance
Lightning Source LLC
Chambersburg PA
CBHW070511090426
42735CB00012B/2737